The Goldfish Window

The Goldfish Window

poems

Lisa Beech Hartz

GRAYSON BOOKS
West Hartford, CT
www.GraysonBooks.com

The Goldfish Window
copyright © 2018, Lisa Beech Hartz
Library of Congress Control Number: 2018937302
published by Grayson Books
West Hartford, CT
printed in the USA

ISBN: 978-0-9982588-9-8

Interior & Cover Design: Cindy Mercier
Cover Art: The Goldfish Window by Childe Hassam
Author photo courtesy of Lincoln Eliot Hartz

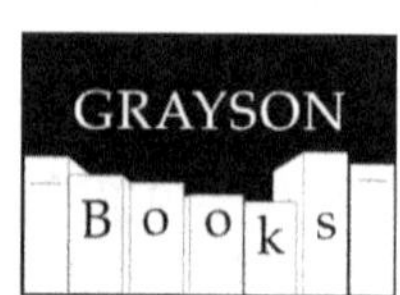

For Ray, always and anywhere. And for our boys,
those endless blessings.

Contents

7

Still Life with Apples

I was almost driven mad tonight,
  Cezanne,
by the apples in the blue bowl
  on our table.
Oh, you should have seen them,
  the sheen
and the dappling. The perfect
  prickles
of the stems. Dazzling, incandescent.
  Helpless,
I was without your brush
  in hand
as they bristled in the bowl made
  bluer
by madder and vermilion. The bruisey
  shadows
and pure white rim.
  I wanted
to call someone.
  To call
my sleeping sons to come open
  their eyes.
Let this life, still, in. To tell them
  not to move,
not to touch these apples.
  Not even once
they brown and soften.
  Not even once
they release their rot-sweet scent.

1

The Boy, Kandinsky, 1876

In Odessa, at summer's end the cello sang scarlet

between his knees, and the piano notes were sugar cubes.

Once, he saw his own voice, a citrine kite, a woodwind

sailing over the Potemkin steps.

Listen, he whispered.

The August street silent at just dusk.

The deep blue slanting light is humming.

Yes, I said. I see.

At the harbor, salt ships and yellow sky.

Don't look, he said. Enter.

Bazille and Monet Leave Paris
by the Garde De L'Est, 1864

On the train, they watch the Seine
weave its way toward Normandy. I follow

their route, fingertrace the map, see them
at Rouen, standing mute before the Delacroix;

its ruby. Its cerulean. The color of their evening
altered, they circle the cathedral twice before retiring.

At Honfleur, Monet leads Bazille up, up
through the narrow cobbled streets he's known

since childhood. Past the complacent villas
and out into the open air. Their eyes take in

the dappled sea, the rocks and trees. White
sails caress the harbor. They love

the sound of their boots shushing
among the grasses. *Fresh. Yes. Yes.*

They love the muscle and pull
of the painting, the effort of it. The will

of the body. *This country is paradise,*
Bazille writes his mother. *Nowhere*

could you find more lush fields with more beautiful trees.
He wants to wrap them in his long arms,

carry them home. This is pure feeling.
They rent two rooms above a bakery. Sugar-

scent between them as they sleep.
In the cool blue mornings,

they rise through the spangled
air, climb to that repose of rock.

They paint from five in the morning
until eight in the evening. They don't speak;

their union in the bloom of color
they press into their canvasses.

Bazille has a smile that invites
and turns you away. Monet

is always short of money. Too soon,
Bazille's body, duty-spent, will lay in a battlefield

for three nights before his father
can retrieve him. Monet

will live long enough to enchant,
deplete and bury Camille;

remarry. Grow a white beard. Complain
of rheumatism in the rain. Spot

Giverny from a train. But just
then, when it was easy to imagine

their azure youth a permanence
like their color-hunger,

there was only the scudding
of the fields, apparition

of the breeze, and their open eyes
in these first days of seeing.

Child Playing: Annette in Front of the Rail-Backed Chair, Edouard Vuillard, 1897

He scrawls the iron bedstead, silent
but for the hush hush now of the pencil,

so that the child forgets him.
She studies the chocolate box he brought her,

its gilded edges. She lifts the lid over and over.
The lid sighs each time she lifts it.

Soon, she'll slide the box into her pocket, save it
to hold very small found things. Special pinks,

marvelous oranges. A green too vaporous to name.
He will paint her dress turquoise, cream.

All else looming. Aching slates and ashes. There
and not there. She doesn't know she must be

herself and two more. Are the dead ones here?
The sharp scent of oil will shift as it dries, an echo

of itself and this longing. Is this love,
the calibrated wish to capture and transform?

And how are we to know when a love has ended?
The child had forgotten him, as he had intended.

Thrummed off to some other interior.

Self-Portrait, Caterina Van Hemessen, 1548

> *I, Caterina Van Hemessen, painted myself in 1548 at the age*
> *of 20.* —Artist's Inscription

The iced silence in the room
but for my own breath, a pulse
cloud, and the brushstrokes like slippered
footsteps on the stair. The chill
that slows the oils. The weighted
sleeve and the light there—
a hoarfrost gleaming.

Then the bonnet containing the face
which blurs, returns, blurs
again as I study it: distant, aglow
as the moon. Soon I will sketch
a quiver of brushes in my other hand.
So much more to say. So many
more moons to reach for.

Berenice Abbott Arrives in New York, 1918

Marriage is the finish for women
who want to do their work.

To be let alone.

Let go. Mother said:
If you're going, go.

Apron strings—ha.
She never had them. Umbilical
tendencies.

Back home Ohio in winter
the snow iced over & me
and Hazel would walk across
the glass across a sea of white threatening
to swallow us up for a too heavy step.

Careful, Hazel always said.

Her eyes even then studied
the horizon. No, I'll never know
that life she chose.

Domestic.

The city with its stratifications—
its clean lines that slice
the woman out of the would be
wife—
promised me nothing.

That, I could believe.

Even the bare trees of Washington Square
can't compete with the window window
window call of the skyline.

Sky line.

My breath boxed in this cold room. Idle
Monday and no coal.

Back home,
which was never home,
the coal cars have frozen to the tracks.
The drifts chase the miners away.

While here on this first day—
the mercury at 7 below—
here, I don't wait to be asked.

I answer.

Edward Steichen Comes to Meet the Master, Stieglitz, New York City, 1900

New York City is horseshit coal smoke organ grinder trolley
scream cop whistle crosswalk *FIORES FIORES* flint in your eye

a push from behind ragman side street clothesline snapping slapping
in the breeze a woman calls *dee dee ay, Didier.* Ragtime saloon

beer steam Bjorncrantz says: fancy a cool one? but I don't
want to be inside anything ever again on a rain washed

morning in early spring outsider in wonderland a girl
with a pale blue ribbon in her hair turns a corner

taking my heart with her kerosene coffee ash a fat man in a hansom
devouring a cigar city of Morgan and Cosa Nostra

Bjorncrantz sees it first my poster one hundred times
the size I made it adorning the entire side of a building

the girl I drew curled into the enormous letter C
dreaming *They work while you sleep* I see

I have been here in fact since before I arrived
everything ahead of itself faster than the eye can catch it

pouring in from everywhere filling the island like a vessel spilling
into the Hudson into the East River into the twentieth century

Stieglitz makes me promise always the camera
what else can I say but yes

Meanwhile, Jacob Lawrence, 1930

Meanwhile, Jacob Lawrence,
aged thirteen, works
his consoling patterns
in a center called Utopia,
in the colony of Harlem. Square,
square, triangle,
triangle. He paints
the triangles red, the squares
blue. Primary colors –
the ones from which all
the others will come.

Is he making sense
of the too-much, too-
many of this city after
fostering and waiting, waiting
so long? Too many bodies. More
faces than can be known.
The clamoring insistence
of the streetcar. Clang,
rush, clatter,
clatter. The people caught
up, carried along.

Someday, street scenes.

But here, now,
in a basement room
of the New York Public Library,
135th and Lenox,
with Toussaint L'Ouverture leaning
over his shoulder (he can feel
the strong hand weighting there) Jacob
Lawrence, aged thirteen, works,
works his own, his own
way, his own way out.

Portrait of José Clemente Orozco, Doris Ulmann, 1929

When she asks me to remove my spectacles,
I am wary, feel as if she is asking me to reveal

a wound. The lenses
a closed window between what I have seen

and what I can show her. Populations
in my mind, writhing. Outside, Park Avenue

slides by, motor purring. *The hand*, she says.
How did that loss change you?

She has the kind of simmering stillness
that permits the question. *It was all right,*

I say. *Once I remembered what remained.*
I raise my one hand and hold it

aloft. The thumb and fingers form
a circle. A third eye burning.

2

Child on a Blue Cushion, Mary Cassatt, 1881

The child's eyes are weighted
with sleep, or sorrow. Some half-
remembered grief. His hands a blur
of uselessness. There's nothing he can do.

Little strange being. Seer, rune.
Not held but suspended, presented. A jewel.
The child knows, what? Cassatt
won't let him look at me.

Outside, the camellias give up their petals
one by one. Like that spring, a loss.
An offering. Where did your grief go, Ray,
my intimate? My familiar?

Your eyes give nothing away.

But I, years on, still hear the sound I made,
the surrender. Is that you?
I said, and said again. Is that you?
No child appeared, nor you.

All Cassatt's babies have eyes like coins
waterworn in a fountain.
Wishes, wishes.

You in your silver car wound, wound,
winding down all the lanes between possibility
and me. Careening in the clear blue quiet
of just before knowing.

Cezanne in Aix, 1866

A man can live on poetry alone in fine weather,
he writes. Wood lark. Blue rock thrush. Two-tailed

pasha butterfly. Nightjar emerging from the bracken.
For some days now, a determined rain.

Bleak dawn, blackened evening. Beneath
all this: tamped grasses, red soil. Limestone

shell. Very soon, the mistral. Cleansing wind.
Nightfishing with Delphin in the tidal pools.

Field scent, harmony. Sleep of the earth.
It's easier all this, than painting, he writes.

But it doesn't lead far.

Once, he leaned among the bastards arguing Ingres
in the overlit café. His trousers held up with string.

Now, when he drinks he sees spirits
swaying just beyond his reach. Dancing,

dancing. Enough to smash everything.
Outside the Provençal trees hum

their secrets. The sun eases across the rasping
field. Stifling room. Infinite placements. Fabric

crests and spurs. The ginger jar, inconstant
muse. All dissipates, moves on. Death

murmurs from ear to hand. The pear
breathes green, thrums against the apple

balanced on a coin. Dapple viridian. Layer
the body in. This vermilion tips the sable brush.

What's known of Nature? Membrane
over membrane. Veil upon veil. Life composed

of a series of screens. Clouds without abruption.

The day diffuses. No pleasure in this labor. Salt
scent under creeping evening. What lies within?

Nothing. Perhaps everything.
Everything, do you see?

The Harbor at Lorient, Berthe Morisot, 1869

Beyond the seawall,
dusk. Tethered boats
hover just above the water
mirror. Take my hand.

Behind us, the fields may
spring with lavender. Unblinking
cottages may hold fast to shore.

But the boats, faithful
mirages, insist, will us
out to sea.

The girl in her white dress—
weightless
as a whim—the wind
might carry her away.

Still inlet. Reflected sky.
Which am I? And what
makes you so sure?

Georgia O'Keeffe Recuperates in Bermuda, 1933

Her dreams are rashes of color, a heart
stream of crash and weep. In the pastel

morning she considers the banyan tree, naked
roots reaching. Last year, the Camaguey

threatened to take the canopies off all the trees
in the Caribbean, but these are the knitted limbs

a hurricane couldn't undo. The banyan,
that strangler fig. Ghosted host missing from its center.

Who lives there now? Black rat, feral cat. Soon
she will return to her body. The breezing leaves

are whispering. Soon the forsaken mind
will widen like an eye and the light will steal

its way in again. But for now there is the banyan tree,
the banana flower, the hot pink hibiscus, and in

the violet dusk the staccato sandpipers along the shore—
a bruising seduction back to the living world.

Stieglitz Recuperates at Lake George, 1902

Stieglitz, reposing on the veranda, contemplates

oblivion. The uncooperative clouds absent themselves,

and even the inconstant breeze thwarts him.

At least a great blue heron eases along

the coastline, hungry. Surveying. Emmy

blathers at the child in the shadowed hall.

Her voice an unstoppable spill. Like the winding

vine consuming the house's façade. When should one

surrender to the part of the mind which says surrender?

Nothing can happen here.

Emmy will bring cups of tea. Hush the child. Call:

Raspberries today, when the grocer's boy has been.

Hasn't he made himself clear? Hasn't he? The heron

fishes now at the edge of the lake, stands motionless.

He has all day. The heavy leaves of the black ash in mid-July,

dusted with summer also wait. They are fully realized

and have nothing left to do but fall.

The Pilgrim Van Gogh, 1879

He arrives near Christmas, speaks to them of Jesus,
the mustard seed, the barren fig tree.

He comes to them in their shanties and sheds,
huts and stables. He follows them down into the mine,

lays his hand on the coal seam. They are struck
by his translucent eyes, the artlessness of his gaze.

Think of God as a workman, he says, *with a face
lined with fatigue, sorrow and suffering.* They listen,

and murmur in their patois. By early spring,
they hear Vincent has given away his books, his boots.

They say he eats now only crusts of bread. He thins,
his eyes burn. He says: *The gospel teaches us to be meek,*

humble of heart. He says: *Your poverty is sublime.*
He blesses their newborns. Waits with the women

at the driftmouth. Forgives their dead. He attends
to the feverish, the damaged. He abandons

his cottage for a shack, relinquishes his bed. They say
he lays himself out like a corpse on cold stones.

He looks for faith everywhere. Stillborn child, mangled
limb. Honeycomb. He speaks now of the mystical body,

supplication, the caged bird. The bones in his face
emerge. *This is what his god asks of him*, they whisper,

*while our god is feckless. Sends us this dreamer
who will bring flowers, when what we need is bread.*

3

The Diver, Paul Cezanne, 1867-1870

Cezanne's diver throws herself outside the frame.
What is she is trying to escape?

I never knew. And that moon, silent witness,
is that you?

Goodbye, goodbye, the diver calls
to the whitewater, never plunging in.

Cezanne's divers evolved into bathers
after all. That is, in later years.

Sometimes I call to you from that other side—
suspended.

Once, for lack of you I threw a wineglass,
marvelous diver

into the stone cold empty bath
to hear the shatter, smash.

Remains:
a thousand muted stars and daggers.

We could just lie down,
you said, in the wreckage.

Oh, but the splash, my darling.
Oh, but the echo.

Nude Against Daylight, Pierre Bonnard, 1908

She has the look of a wild bird, its swift
surveillance. Luminous. A quiver

of refractions in this low-slung room.
I sketch just briefly. Paint

from memory. Striations of color. Crimson
over carmine. A jasper hue. In the pink house

among the trees, over and over, I paint her. Opaline,
iridescent as she rises from the bath. Her body's

proximity a rhythm pulsing through me. Outside,
constant mimosa, olive tree. Mauve shimmer

of the Esterel. Here, kestrel. Changeling.
A thousand glints, glazes compose

the mosaic of her skin. I paint want
from satiety. Conjure it up from across

the hours. It will go on like this for years.
Though the evening falls, jeweled and absolute.

Vuillard at Villenueve, 1897

In her crowded rooms he sat
tethered, conversation undulating
through him. Ambitions and sensualities.

This art. These pretensions. His
acute awareness
of the exquisite drape of her dress.

Once,
out under her indigo sky
she took his hand.

In that moment, he saw
the exact color of the cooling
riverbank and beyond it, the silver

birches pooling shadow. Vibrant
grasses. Her shuttered house.

They were alone. Two distinct figures
in a festooned and ruined landscape.

Study of Lilia, Carolus-Duran, 1887

When the entire woman
can be found at the place
where her throat meets her shoulder,

in that fresh inch,
it doesn't matter
that you can't see her face.

Or that her lips—
which you are certain are full,
small, a rosette, a perfect berry—

are not in view. Then,
when the woman can be
contained in this way,
there is only the curve

of her lily neck, the rush
of her amber hair as it reaches
for the clip, an anchor lost

in the glints that catch the strands.
Only the porcelain ear and pink
crescent of back, luminous.

Too soon, she will turn and fix on you
her near-black eyes, her gaze
that holds too much, and there is so much

you don't want to know.
Keep still, keep still, this can be
all there is. This can be why. Even
if you won't remember.
So many years later.

Camille on her Deathbed, Claude Monet, 1879

He takes up the brush, sketches quickly as the light recedes,
as the face transforms. He recalls the girl in the garden,

in the poppy field. Within the green dress, under the parasol,
the sheer white veil. From him she learned how to keep still.

How to lean without seeming to lean. How to live
on scraps. How to ask. How to wear fine clothes.

How to take them off. Does he whisper in her cooling
ear? Imagine she would say yes. *Oh,*

yes. All that matters is the work
which will outlast us both.

Letitia Felix, Clarence H. White, 1901

You never tell her to hold still. Never
tell her how to compose herself

or where to lay her hands though
you see they appear to be reaching,

hesitating. Just shy of touching.
You don't ever ask her

what she is feeling. Your presence
translucent, a screen between

what she has to show you
and what you want to be shown. A girl,

waiting. Not knowing she is just three years
from marriage, seven from her first child.

Her opaque gaze; the lay of her arms.
Hands hesitate, reach, beseech. But wait.

Withholding. She thinks nothing
will ever happen to her.

She'll never leave Ohio, never
see beyond that stand of beeches.

Even her mouth, undecided.
Here she is—

unfinished as the sentence
just forming on her lips.

Schiele Has Left His Subject in a Curious State of Suspension, 1918

As my belly swells he asks for me less
and less. I wait outside his battered door.

I listen. *You are supreme to me*, I write,
and study him until his images

tattoo themselves across my mind—
strands of blue-black ink: crooked

spine, hipbone jutting, cruel line
of the famished thigh. Wasted

nakedness. And beyond it,
the impossibility of intimacy.

The very existence of the body
does not permit it. His subjects,

relics, artifacts, remains
of some inscrutable experiment.

Across his surfaces wrought, wrenched.
Always he takes what he needs. Adele, Gerti.

Me. Splays us open. Spreads our legs
until they're nearly split. Paints

our hearts there. Twists
our arms with his pencil, with his black

crayon. Jagged line, fevered complacency. Silent
commotion, a spectacle of empty limb.

The indigo skirt flows against itself.
The ivory underclothes split.

Compass rose, from above. Meanwhile,
the baby defies him with its quickening.

The Rebecca Portraits, Paul Strand, 1917-1932

What she wanted most was to be seen.
He leaned her back against a tree.

Hold still, he said, *two minutes. Maybe
three.* This is what the photos say,

and this. Limits of beauty, tenderness.
Three minutes. Sometimes four.

He laid her out on the lino floor.
What she wanted most was to be

seen. Who would she love, and how
would she know? Silver button,

blinded eye. Idle she is, and so bereft.
The stages of learning are limited

to the practice you invest. Mostly,
she wanted to be seen.

Ruined summer turns to spring.
Read this life backwards, please.

Begin with endings, sleeping pills. Colcha
stitch. Her without him. First the pupil,

then the iris painted in. You see the image
from the other side, from across that glass

divide. The photos may be turned more ways
than one. He did intend this loss of ground.

And she was waiting to be seen.

Untitled [Girl with a Bow], Doris Ulmann, 1933

At Lang Syne, that flatland,
Julia introduces her Negroes

as the people who came
with the acres. Like fruit trees

or pests. Like the Spanish moss
that seems to exist

on a diet of air. They have
the blackest black eyes

that keep everything inside.

I feel weightless,
a shimmer.

Julia's red hair stands out
from her head like a terrible crown.

You can see she's torn about them.

And not torn.

Chin up, eyes down.

I say, *I'd like to take your picture.*

Why *take?*

Blink, blink,
say the children.

A cicada-filled silence.

The mother on the porch,
rocking. Same spot
her mother rocked.

Her grandmother.

Same spot some day
her spindly daughter.

Outside the Heaven's Gate,
leaning: Little dark brown girl.

Hairbow like magnolia blossom.
Outsized, waxen, glowing.

Indigo skirt. Sky blue ruffled
blouse. Iridescent buttons.

Silver earrings.

She's seen my big camera
inside the church.

And me, the odd, sparrow
woman standing next to it.

Watching as they dropped
to their knees and keened:

Flood come a creepin o'er our door.

She looks straight through me
and beyond into the palmetto

scrub scrim.
I say: *You're blooming.*

How close will she let me get?

She holds something
burnished inside herself. A stone.

Are you a little flower?

Shimmer of a smile
in her eyes.

When I was a girl, I say,
I liked to imagine I was a rose.

I swing my white
skirt. Petals breezing.

I won't ask you to smile, I say.

The little stone inside her shifts.

You just be there, I say.
And I'll be here.

The care her mother has taken.

The hands that tied
the bow. Stitched on
those oyster buttons.

She studies the other children who
gather and scatter. Skittish, half-

curious. They play shadow tag.
They play crack-the-whip.

4

The Firefly, George Seeley, 1910

What might this girl tell me? Cleft chin, collar bone.
The desolation in her eyes. With all her losses

she seems to have arrived from the glow
behind, carrying with her this small memento

of where she's been. Because we do not see
the entire bowl she holds,

the gaping bowl seems not to end.
The bowl she'll drop this token into,

into its open mouth, where it will go on
falling, falling, never touching down.

The photo, a clue. Proof
and not proof at all. Carbon negative

pressed to copper plate. Acid baths etch
to the desired depth, determine

relative darkness. I love this language.
The relative darkness of this photogravure:

very dark with glimpses of a way out,
into the light. The firefly may not be

a firefly at all, but a pearl, a coin.
Some manipulation

of the negative creating a glowing orb
held between thumb and finger, echoing

the jeweled headband. A softer glow behind
the girl, a lit lamp in an abandoned room.

The Sick Child, Edvard Munch, 1885-1926

Father says I'm watching
from the other side.

But he can't tell you
how. You don't remember

my voice. You remember
the cough ratcheting. The bedside

untouched glass of water. The pillow
white-framing. Cage

weight-ribbed. Palm-bloody.
You remember my hair the color

of calamity. My eyes
the color of smoke.

I am cloud.
I cover your sky.

Vuillard and Misia in the Rue du Depart, 1909

Washed over by the clamor and splash of the afternoon café,

he watches her with opaque eyes. The cigarette sighs

in his nicotine beard. The table, a stone between them, rests

on thinly wrought legs. The chair seems barely to contain her.

Her hips ache, she says. As if she has come a long way

through many streets. How can an absence be

so heavy, he thinks. Just beyond the soft resignation

of her shoulders, the lovely gray light illuminates

the café window. Its glow a halo. Her hard, little mouth

settles into its downward curve. She speaks, and her words fall,

dropped coins in an empty tray. *I am not what you want*,

she says. *A long time ago, yes, many years. As a child*

requires a cake behind glass. How startled he is; how

slapped. He lights another cigarette to occupy his hands.

Beauty has undraped itself from her, he thinks. Like a lover

will in sleep. Leaving only a sorrow of reminiscence.

Her fingers flit along the table's edge. Her voice

smoke. She trembles almost imperceptibly. She was

exquisite. She was desire. Then, from across the room

the crash of a glass, shattering. The patrons

silenced by that violence. It seems to him to contain everything;

that rupture. He doesn't speak, remembering he was once

drawn to the vulnerable nape of her neck, but fell in love

with the silver bell of her earring. Its stubborn silence.

The voices rise again to fill the void.

The Enchanted Garden,
John William Waterhouse, 1916

Azure as it was in Rome. Oppressive, remote,
sublime. The color blue against the skin.

The mythic tale the skin tells. The ancient tattoo.
Circe and Echo. Always echo. No pain

but haggard. So haggard and so woebegone. *Nino,*
his mother called, her voice cerulean. Her dress

a hem of cockleshells. His father said she'd flown
to Avalon. His tears not dropping but suspended,

crystalline. Consumption. The heroic cut
to his shoulders gone. London sun, midwinter

white, the gloaming in his rooms. The child's face,
unfinished. The imprecision of age, he thinks.

What is outside us, what is within. Camellia,
foxglove, rhododendron. The oil-scent

intoxicates. The cancer whispers
in the outer room. Merciful cold,

merciful darkness. Merciful Keats
and Tennyson. The comfort of a well-

learned passage, a well-worn corridor.
Yes, the flowers.

What remains. Composed from memory. In the garden
the roses bloom. And beyond them, snow.

The Orchard, Clarence H. White, 1902

You have learned to wait. And not
to wait. To arrive in silence. To listen

for the image as much as to see it.
It will appear to you in the scent

of the early apples in the orchard.
In the shushing of the three skirts

across the grass. This morning
you can't locate the picture.

No matter how your eyes scan
the frame. Then, the sensation

of helplessness. Of a severing
of access to a kind of god.

The one who whispers in the dark-
room as the shadows emerge. The tree

blackened with damp. Your wife's velvet
jacket. How one leaf glows white

among the fallen fruit and one
appears to be an absolute absence

of light. You wait and watch,
heart trilling. Hand

on the lens cap. Listen
for the birds. Name them:

starling, waxwing. Swallow. Somehow
when you reach that precise moment

their twitter and lash will burn them-
selves into the glass. The women's hum

and chatter. The water-scent filling
the shade. Then, the sunlight

beyond; how it dazzles
the grass. How it invites

like the open sea.
Middle ground:

her two sisters in their dark
dresses turning like the workings

of a clock. Offering
poses and poses.

Have patience.
Soon enough they will forget.

Meanwhile, the spangled ground,
the crushed and tender leaves.

Meanwhile, the anticipated
moment of release. Your wife

and everything contained in her
turns in her white skirt, reaches

down for the waiting apple.
You hardly know you've done it

'til it's done.
Light floods the lens.

5

Still Life, Henri Fantin-Latour, 1866

Consider the tender flesh of the orange,
this orange, the one he's split open to please you—

releasing its lush, percussive scent. Remember
what came before the threaded membrane burst,

when to imagine tasting the ruptured interior
of an orange in midwinter was its own seduction.

Even the flowers. Even the teacup, the closed book.
All else still, complicit in this unlacing.

Paula Modersohn-Becker Holds Her Newborn
for the First Time, 1907

Bauble, bébé, thief. You
began as an ache in the back
of my throat. Something left
unsaid. The place you grew from
fills, refills. The womb awash.
We women reside inside
our failures,
shelter-grateful.

Before your pate dries,
I know the hues.

Annie—My First Success,
Julia Margaret Cameron, 1864

In Calcutta, that riot of hues, the walled-
in garden parties were weighted
with marigolds and the women wore

camellias in their hair. Their pinks glowed
divine as the mango sun
flared over West Bengal. Here,

the muted spectrum of an English
midwinter afternoon forgives
the camera its grey-tone limits

and I do manage to arrest the refractions
and energies of the child just in

from the frosted garden. The silent
white sky still streaked

in her hair that lights
the ivory button I carried

from Murshidabad. An unease
in her eyes as the day fades.

Meanwhile in the City of Joy,
they prepare for monsoon.

Triangles, Imogene Cunningham, 1928

Light pooled. The girl, poured. Cream.
A candle, resonating. Her body

closed around her. The unclaimed space
at her center. The pealing ring from there.

It's all right being locked in if it's a garden
and the magnolia blooms.

Light pooled. Poured. Pealing.

Later, when I was free, I did other things.

Portrait of the Herbalist, Lang Syne Plantation, Doris Ulmann, 1929

Leaves, roots, blooms. Heal
the wound. Chase the curse. Spell it

back again. Mojo hand, conjure bag.
Green flannel for money. White for baby.

I collect the pieces in the sack
according to your need. Frog eye,

honeycomb. Fingernail, bat wing. Orchid
root for lucky hand. Swallow heart for love.

Breathe on it. Bring it life. Soak it
in whiskey. In piss. In jizz.

Hide it between your skirt
and your sex. It is alive

with spirit. O sinner, O mourner.
There is nothing between you

and this earth. There is everything
between you and this earth.

Fill the honey jar. Put the name inside.
Love cannot resist you now.

The Heart of the Storm, Anne Brigman, 1902

Juniper, zephyr, woman.
The longing a pull in the lung.

Thunderhead pink on the horizon. Air,
thin, shifts. Moonscape tells us

to go home: We root. Sharp light,
savior, slices the woman

from the searing sky. The muscled
pine. Her every curve

a kind of armor. We have now
traveled too far to be found.

6

Clarence H. White, Edward Steichen, 1903

It's the portrait of you by Steichen, the 1903, that does it. Makes me
want to tell you all my secret sorrows. Share my sense

of wonder. Let you share yours. Art solace for losses sustained
and anticipated. I see the weight of it in your eyes, and in

every image you burned. What would you tell me, Clarence
H. White, if I asked you about art-passion and how for so many

it eats away love to the bone? They call it genius if it's Stieglitz,
or Hemingway. Oh, but the wreckage they left behind.

The ransacked landscapes. You left behind only one wife,
Jane, whose face you made beautiful with light and glass.

Copper. Platinum and gum bichromate. Three sons.
I've seen them on the shores of Maine among the rocks

and myths. You know the slow pull in the heart when you
look at them. The way you can only hold yourself back

as they come into being. Only watch them fade away
into their own, separate futures. My own boys

leave me a little every day. I want to ask you about that.
How you solved the problem of time.

And when you felt yourself ending in Mexico City,
what, if anything, did you regret?

Edge of the Woods—Evening,
Clarence H. White, 1900

You plan your images all week in your mind—

how to spend the one pane of glass you can afford.

In the little office at the back of the store you sit with your numbers,

but all the while the pictures take shape. Dangle

over your adding machine, breeze over your bowed,

balding head. How the woods will appear in all their dappling

weightlessness; inviting. How the girl will turn. How

the light will keen her profile. How it will seem

that she's turned back to face you, to tell you something

essential before she disappears. Not asking anything of you.

Not asking you to come with her, certainly, past that

first dazzling branch—the one you spotted that told you:

this is where the eye begins. Even the fog will cooperate.

Hover in the middle distance. Contain all the whisperlight

of the gloaming. The crescent of skin a kind of leaf-

echo and the white cuff. Even the tall grasses, singing,

will have something to say.

Couple Wearing Raccoon Coats with a Cadillac, Taken on West 127th Street, James Van Der Zee, 1932

These are the marvelous unseen.
She in her sugared fur doubling

the size of her. The so long
car he has just entered.

Are they asking you along?

The smooth, cool shine of the fender,
the white-walls. How the grill gleamed

mercury when I asked it to.
And all the shades pulled down

in all the windows looking on.
Total absence of audience,

if not for me.
You're welcome.

And if the brown faces surprise you,
why don't you come uptown
and see for yourself?

Now Comes Mary Cassatt Down
Auguste Renoir's Garden Path, 1919

Renoir, folded into his wheelchair,
placed inside his little glass house.

There beyond the lavender, he watches her,
his brush clutched in one bound, rheumatic hand.

Cassatt wears a capacious, tea-colored straw hat,
eyes blind as mirrors.

Armand, shadow servant, guides her sylph-
slender sleeve. Noonlight blazes her blue dress,

intemperate turquoise of an Algerian sky.
Her hat floats like a peregrine,

like the swift brown end of summer.
In Algiers, years ago, Renoir watched

the Barbary light transform the rags
of a distant beggar into the robes of a prince.

But this is August, 1919. Degas is dead.
Renoir's Aline is dead.

Things fall away, Renoir thinks.
The discovery of light turned our heads.

Cassatt's narrow step wakes the sand-colored stones.
The rock roses reach for her hem.

Renoir looks again to the easel.

Our most wise pictures are made of what we do not know,
he thinks. *We obscure, the better to illuminate.*

She arrives at his door.

We only begin to understand.

Underwater Swimmer, Andre Kertesz, 1917

At Galicia, we heard the Russians
shouting *brzo, brzo*—

and in the distortion of the juniper
breeze, I heard my other tongue.

At Esztergom, half-
paralyzed by memory, I watched

the tender contorted wade into the therapy pool,
like worshippers into baptismal waters—

with terror, with reverence. I wanted
to be rid of myself. I wanted

to be annihilated there.
What water can do,

this war has done:
overwhelmed and cleansed us.

Submerging
all boundaries, landscapes. Rushing

histories toward a vanishing.
But then the boy

(so like you, Jeno, I thought
for a moment, *brother*) crossed

the ice-white tile, surefooted
and flung his youth into the cool.

Looking into the depths,
through the elliptic trickery of waves,

I watched his head disappear.
I captured this. I saw

how beautiful it was.
And I remembered afternoons

at shallow Balaton,
where running through the grass

fleetfoot for the lake, you (Jeno,
brother) seemed to spread wings.

Worpswede Peasant Child Sitting on a Chair,
Paula Modersohn-Becker, 1905

This wisp, eyes dark as secrets. Amber
hair, dark-winter shift. The days

parceled out in bits of string. Counting
the chrysanthemums. Ghosted

handprints on the windowpane. Pocketed
box. Inside:

pebble, petal, silvered mothwing. Yesterday,
she picked all the warm, blue-black grapes

she could reach. Their ink stained her pale
pink lips. Little thief, little bandit.

Sweet-juice intoxicated. The vines
left naked, bereft.

Madame Cezanne Exhibition, The Metropolitan Museum of Art, New York City, January 2015

She's with me all day after that.
In the park, watching

the puffy coats like bright poppies
slipping down the snowy

embankments on their little disks.
She shadows me

down the shiny avenues and iced
streets and even into MOMA

where I could hear her skirts swishing
through the galleries. Her voice smoky

when she used it, which wasn't
often. She has very small things to say.

Such a red. Too many lines. They say
he spent long minutes

between brushstrokes,
contemplating each one. The halting

greens and blues. And the drawings, too.
A million million tiny lines. How long

she must have held the pose regardless
of the sudden noise from the street,

the buzzing fly. How wise her eyes.
And all the permutations in them.

In the evenings, when his brain had sunk
to glowing ash,

she read to him. Sometimes, yes,
until the candle drowned.

7

Falling Blue, Agnes Martin, 1963

Iridescent mist, components of a cloud. We surrender

to this enchantment, fixed and glittering as a sequin.

Our years spangle now in memory. Dots, dashes. Nimbo-

stratus, cumulonimbus. Today, the rain comes so swiftly.

Urgency of midsummer. Drenching us, a million mirrored

drops. That dappling only understood from some

unattainable distance. Yes, the water will recede, feed

the streams, the rivers. O, but the rush and pooling. O,

but the diamonds left winking among the leaves.

Untitled, Joan Mitchell, 1956

Slashy pines and peely birches—
water-scent and storm
coming, the pines lean and heave
and the birches give up their leaves
in bits and flutters—

in coppers and ochres. Cloud
seeping into violet and maybe
hail. The year hesitates, yearning,
between the buckling house unseen
and the lake vast and fleeting
as a season becomes horizon
and no other shore.

The waves will leave her salt-
lipped and kiss-hungry soon
enough. The dune grasses
will sway, smear and spur. Rush
of sand-spray-splatter.

Wait here? Or crash into rain?

Even now as she reaches the wind
picks up and spans the void.

Right After, Eva Hesse, 1969

Filaments of fiberglass cling
to your nesting hands. A density
of implication. Who says
yes, and why? Say
your name. Capture
its history. Another country.

You recall your mother's scent
but not her face. The flutter
of her fingers through
your hair. Music like the tapping
of spoon on glass. A mirror.

Immediate. Somewhere dusk returns
and the birds white-feather the tall trees.

Here, rain. Who will comfort you now?
Who?

River Bathers, Grace Hartigan, 1961

I see them. Is this the game? How many of them are
there? Which ones count? The ones who swam

away from me, who echo now at stop lights
and coming home early evening—

Crossing the James at dusk breaks me up,
and the Western Branch of the Elizabeth. Count

the flecks and glazes the breeze makes. Let
the eye shift then into now. There were nine.

Four survived. Here, there are suggestions of boys who lived
long enough to step into the stream without holding

their mother's hand. See how the water buffets and
primes. See how distance and light combine.

Jacob's Ladder, Helen Frankenthaler, 1957

We can't know what we're making
when we're making it, even
if it's love. Even in the half-
light, time conflates, contains
all the bodies we've ever been.

We move with no intent
but intention. We dip
and swallow. Stroke—
scrawl—
dash.

We are the fluid line,
unprimed. We rise.

Ode to Forgetting, Louise Bourgeois, 2002

The echo on the other side, stitch-scratch and red line:
clues. What's the worst that could happen? I'd ask you

not to leave, but you're not leaving. Louise says:
I had a flashback of something that never existed.

You wake me in the dark to say goodbye then
haunt the house all day so I'll miss you. Whisper

anecdotes from our early days, and I listen. Artifacts
and accumulations embroider the imagination. Louise

kept every blouse, every dress she ever owned.
A fabric ephemera (detritus?) of remembrance.

She had an assistant named Jerry, and a seamstress.
I like the idea of them arriving each morning like meaning,

like inspiration. The workshop festooned
with possibility. With burlap and buckram

and tulle. With every cruel or kind gesture gathered
across a lifetime. Every stain, every scorch mark

incorporated. What forgetting feels like. A scrim
between your self and your self, impenetrable

and translucent. I have trouble letting go when we're finished.
Is that why? Meanwhile, the ghost of Louise

in her studio, amassing. You bring me another
cup of coffee, trace of sugar a lacing on the rim.

Breeze Rushing Through Fall Flowers,
Alma Thomas, 1966

I read flowers, but I see stones, like the rock

fences, vine-strapped and sapling-studded

that lapped the backcountry roads of my girl-

hood. A mosaic of trial and error. Tessera

puzzles. Inscrutable glyphs of granite chip

to chip. No mortar, magic. And the fissures

white as sighs. They say Miss Thomas painted

with a bird's eye view. If true, look, look. There

we are just off-canvas in your father's little French

car – winding, winding. All the colors of the fall

flowers of New England: red clover; yellow wood-

sorrel; purple coneflower; amber aster; tendrilled, tow-

headed witch hazel glazing the roadside like so much hope.

Untitled [July '75], Helen Frankenthaler, 1975

Wash of grey sky undecided. White
moonhover. Horizon ablaze and the blue

streak and cobalt. White froth rising. Yellow
bird submerged. What does orange mean?

Rush away and wave. You're always
leaving. How far this time? Is that

enough? Did you even hear me? Is that
black, and which way is it moving?

I don't know what moonpull is, only
that to look too long is an opening

to falling, and the tide is game
and ready for anything.

The Goldfish Window, Childe Hassam, 1916

In the yellow morning she combs her fingers through
the knots the night's rocking has left in her hair.

A dozen strands form an amber cloud. She steps
to the open window and offers it to the breeze

which spirits it away. Nesting season. Perhaps
she'll see those strands again. Water murmurs

in the bowl. Light ripple and goldflash. An unseen
bird flirts from the shadowed camellia. Bruised

petals, pinestraw. The nest, the one the birdsong is conjuring:
an open cup of surrendered woven things.

Notes on the Poems

Child Playing: Annette in Front of the Rail-backed Chair, Edouard Vuillard, 1897: Annette is the daughter of Vuillard's sister, Marie, whose disastrous marriage to Vuillard's closest friend, Ker-Xavier Roussel produced three children – a stillborn child in 1894, a son born in August of 1896 who died within months of his birth, and Annette, who was deeply cherished by her uncle.

Self-Portrait, Caterina Van Hemessen, 1548: This painting has been identified as the first self-portrait showing an artist, male or female, at work at the easel.

Berenice Abbott Arrives in New York, 1918: The opening stanza is a direct quote from Berenice Abbott as reported in ARTnews: Avis Berman, "The Unflinching Eye of Berenice Abbott," January, 1981.

Edward Steichen Comes to Meet the Master, Stieglitz, New York City, 1900: This poem was inspired by Steichen's own description of his first visit to New York City: "I started off for New York en route to Paris with my friend Carl Bjorncrantz, a member of the Milwaukee Art Students League. The sight of New York, impressive enough, became doubly so when I saw an outdoor advertisement that was designed after one of my postcards for Cascarets. For the company's theme, 'They work while you sleep,' I had painted an attractive young woman asleep, with the 'C' of 'Cascarets' forming her bed. It covered the whole side of a warehouse building six stories high and a block long. I decided then and there that New York must be the art center of the world." —Edward Steichen, *A Life in Photography*

Cezanne in Aix: The opening line is imagined phrasing inspired by lines from a letter Cezanne wrote to Numa Coste dated November 1868 referring to a childhood friend: "M. Paul Aliexis, a boy who is, by the way, far superior and, one can safely say, not stuck up, lives on poetry and other things. I saw him a few times during the fine weather..." The tenth and eleventh lines, in italics, are direct quotes from a letter Cezanne wrote to Emile Zola dated June 30, 1866.

The Pilgrim Van Gogh, 1879: The fourth stanza contains a direct quote from a letter from Van Gogh to his brother, Theo, dated December 26, 1878.

Nude Against Daylight, Pierre Bonnard, 1908: The model for this painting and for many other nudes, in and out of the bath, was Bonnard's wife, Marthe, a favorite subject for decades.

Schiele Has Left His Subject in a Curious State of Suspension, 1918: The title of this poem comes from a caption to the painting, "Portrait of Victor Ritter von Bauer, 1918," found in *Egon Schiele, 1890-1918: Desire and Decay*, by Wolfgang Georg Fischer: "By cropping the feet, Schiele has left his subject in a curious state of suspension."

The Rebecca Portraits, Paul Strand, 1917-1932: These photographs were Paul Strand's attempt to match the artistry of his mentor Alfred Stieglitz's masterful photographs of Stieglitz's wife, Georgia O'Keeffe, and are largely seen as a failure – lacking emotional and sensual resonance. Rebecca Salsbury James married Paul Strand in 1922. After their divorce in 1933, she found her own modes of artistic expression creating reverse paintings on glass and taking part in the revival of the Mexican folk art of colcha stitch embroidery. In 1968, crippled by rheumatoid arthritis and no longer able to create art, she took her own life.

Untitled (Girl with Bow), Doris Ulmann, 1833: Julia Peterkin was the Pulitzer Prize—winning author of *Scarlet Sister Mary*. Peterkin's work focused on the lives of rural African-Americans, though she herself was white. With her marriage she became mistress of Lang Syne Plantation in the Gullah coastal region of South Carolina. In 1933, she collaborated with photographer Doris Ulmann on *Roll, Jordan, Roll*, an exploration of the lives of former slaves and their descendants.

The Sick Child, Edvard Munch, 1885-1926: The Sick Child is a series of works – paintings and engravings – exploring the loss of Munch's sister, Johanne Sophie, to tuberculosis in 1877 when she was fifteen and he was fourteen.

Vuillard and Misia in the Rue du Depart: Misia Godebska Natanson (1872-1950) was muse and model to many artists of Belle Epoque Paris.

Acknowledgments

Thank you to the editors of the following journals in which these poems first appeared, some under different titles.

Blackbird: "The Rebecca Portraits, Paul Strand, 1917-1932;" and "*Triangles,* Imogene Cunningham, 1928"

Catamaran: "Bazille and Monet Leave Paris by the Gare de L'Est, 1864;" "Now Comes Mary Cassatt Down Auguste Renoir's Garden Path, 1919"

Chattahoochee Review: "Egon Schiele Has Left His Subject in a Curious State of Suspension, 1918"

Common Ground: "*Study of Lilia,* Carolus-Duran, 1887"

Crazyhorse: "*Untitled (July '75),* Helen Frankenthaler;" "*Falling Blue,* Agnes Martin, 1963"

Dogwood, A Journal of Poetry and Prose: "Cezanne in Aix, 1895"

The Gettysburg Review: "Stieglitz Recuperates at Lake George, 1902," "*The Orchard,* C.H. White, 1902"

The Massachusetts Review: "Portrait of José Clemente Orozco, Doris Ulmann, 1929"

Mud Season: "The Pilgrim Van Gogh, 1879;" "*Child Playing: Annette in Front of the Rail-Baked Chair,* Edouard Vuillard, 1897;" "Vuillard and Misia in the Rue De Depart, 1909;" "*The Enchanted Garden,* John William Waterhouse, 1916;" "Paula Modersohn-Becker Holds Her Newborn for the First Time, 1907"

PoemMemoirStory: "*Still Life,* Henri Fantin-Latour, 1866"

Poet Lore: "*(Untitled), Girl with Bow,* Doris Ulmann, 1933;" "*Underwater Swimmer,* Andre Kertesz, 1917;" "*Ode to Forgetting,* Louise Bourgeios, 2002"

Redivider: "*Portrait of the Herbalist, Lang Syne Plantation,* Doris Ulmann, 1929"

Subtropics: "The Boy, Kandinsky, 1876"

WomenArts Quarterly Journal: "*The Diver,* Paul Cezanne, 1867-1870"

Thanks to my teachers—especially to Jody Bolz, who always believed.

And to Natasha Trethewey and Kevin Young under whose watchful gaze this collection took its first steps at the magical Postgraduate Writers Conference at Vermont College of Fine Arts.

And always thank you to my sister, Leslie Beech, who is the very best one.

About the Author

Lisa Beech Hartz is executive director of Seven Cities Writers Project, a non-profit that brings creative writing workshops to underserved communities. She currently guides a workshop in a city jail, and a memoir workshop of the Jim Crow Era. This collection, originally titled *Bloom or Perish*, was selected by Mark Doty for the Robert Creeley Prize. She lives in the Tidewater region of Virginia with her husband and four sons.

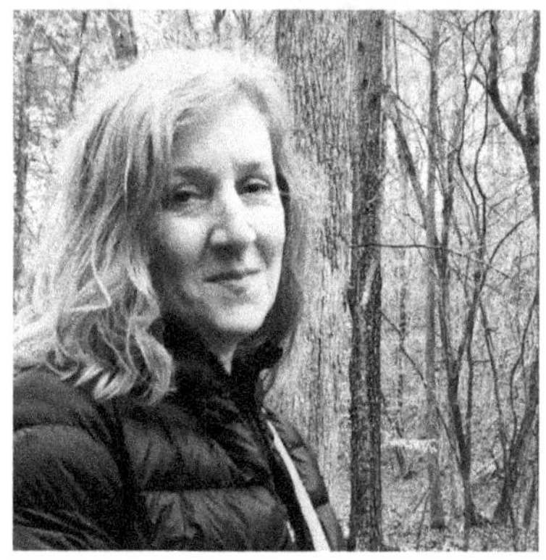

www.ingramcontent.com/pod-product-compliance
Lightning Source LLC
Chambersburg PA
CBHW071455030726
47593CB00003B/1021